word building

In the Kitchen

Word Building with Prefixes and Suffixes

Pam Scheunemann

Consulting Editor, Diane Craig, M.A./Reading Specialist

A Division of ABDO

ABDO
Publishing Company

visit us at www.abdopublishing.com

Published by ABDO Publishing Company, a division of ABDO, P.O. Box 398166, Minneapolis, Minnesota 55439. Copyright © 2013 by Abdo Consulting Group, Inc. International copyrights reserved in all countries. No part of this book may be reproduced in any form without written permission from the publisher. Super SandCastle™ is a trademark and logo of ABDO Publishing Company.

Printed in the United States of America, North Mankato, Minnesota
062012
092012

 PRINTED ON RECYCLED PAPER

Editor: Liz Salzmann
Content Developer: Nancy Tuminelly
Interior Design: Kelly Doudna, Mighty Media, Inc.
Production: Oona Gaarder-Juntti, Mighty Media, Inc.
Photo Credits: Banana Stock, Brand X Pictures, Comstock Images, David Sacks, George Doyle, Hermera Technologies, Jupiterimages, Marc Debnam, Maria Teijeiro, MW, Pixland, Polka Dot images, Shutterstock, Stockbyte, Thinkstock Images

Library of Congress Cataloging-in-Publication Data
Scheunemann, Pam, 1955-
 In the kitchen : word building with prefixes and suffixes / Pam Scheunemann.
   p. cm. -- (Word building)
 ISBN 978-1-61714-966-5
 1. English language--Suffixes and prefixes--Juvenile literature. 2. Vocabulary--Juvenile literature. 3. Language arts (Elementary) I. Title.
 PE1175.S346 2012
 428.1--dc22
                    2010054480

Super SandCastle™ books are created by a team of professional educators, reading specialists, and content developers around five essential components—phonemic awareness, phonics, vocabulary, text comprehension, and fluency—to assist young readers as they develop reading skills and strategies and increase their general knowledge. All books are written, reviewed, and leveled for guided reading, early reading intervention, and Accelerated Reader® programs for use in shared, guided, and independent reading and writing activities to support a balanced approach to literacy instruction.

contents

What Is Word Building? 4

Let's Build Words 6

Emma Is Cooking! 16

Match It Up! 22

Glossary 24

What is Word Building?

Word building is adding groups of letters to a word. The added letters change the word's meaning.

COOKS

Prefix

Some groups of letters are added to the beginning of words. They are called prefixes. Some prefixes have more than one meaning.

Suffix

Some groups of letters are added to the end of words. They are called suffixes. Some suffixes have more than one meaning.

re + cook + ed

prefix + base word + suffix

recooked

The prefix **re** means to do it again.
The base word **cook** means to prepare food.
The suffix **ed** means that the action already happened.
Recooked means that someone prepared the food again.

Let's Build words

bake

Laurie will bake the cookies for 12 minutes.

Zoey has unbaked bread dough.

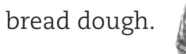

Tim is baking chocolate chip cookies.

unbaked

The prefix **un** means not or opposite.

The suffix **ed** turns the verb into an adjective.

baking

The suffix **ing** means that the action is happening now.

More Words

bakes, baked, baker, bakers, bakery, bakeries, prebaked

～～～ Rule ～～～

When a verb ends with *e*, drop the *e* before adding **ed** or **ing**.

7

roll

Marcus is rolling the dough.

Marcy waits to roll more dough.

rolling

The suffix **ing** means that the action is happening now.

reroll

The prefix **re** means to do it again.

More Words

roller, rollers, unroll, unrolls, unrolling, unrolled, rerolls, rerolling, rerolled, preroll, prerolling, prerolls, prerolled

Ali will reroll the dough until it is just right.

peel

Anna takes the peel off the orange.

Dana removes apple peels with a fancy peeler.

Jon is peeling a carrot.

peels

The suffix **s** means there is more than one.

peeler

The suffix **er** means the person or thing that does the action.

peeling

The suffix **ing** means that the action is happening now.

More Words

peelers, peelings, peeled, unpeeled

11

fry

Andy knows how to fry an egg.

Nathan has refried beans in his taco.

Nikki is frying hamburger meat in a pan.

refried

The prefix **re** means to do it again.

The suffix **ed** turns a word into an adjective.

frying

The suffix **ing** means that the action is happening now.

More Words

fries, fried, fryer

⌇ ⌇ ⌇ Rule ⌇ ⌇ ⌇

When a verb ends with *y*, change the *y* to *i* before adding **ed**.

mix

When all of the milk is added, Jack will mix the batter.

Kelly is using a hand mixer.

Lana is mixing the salad dressing.

mixer

The suffix **er** means the person or thing that does the action.

mixing

The suffix **ing** means that the action is happening now.

More Words

mixes, mixers, mixed, unmixed, remix, remixed, remixing

Emma Is Cooking!

Emma is a crazy cook.

She cooks many things out of a book.

She has things cooking all the time.

Once she even cooked a lime!

17

She preheats the oven
when she wants to bake.
The heat must be just right
for baking a cake.
Emma really cares about
everything she makes.
She is careful not to spill
when making milkshakes!

Emma cooks her soup in a big pot.
She makes healthy food healthier,
and then serves it hot.
Oh, Emma likes to fix foods just right.
I hope she's fixing what I like tonight!

Match It Up!

Choose the word with the correct prefix or suffix to complete each sentence.

1 Tina _____ the oven.
  a. preheated
  b. heating

2 Cindy is _____ dough in the blue bowl.
  a. mixing
  b. premixed

3 Mike and Gaby are good _____.

    a. uncooked

    b. cooks

4 Sophia is happy when the cookies are _____.

    a. baked

    b. bakes

5 Jack and Jen have _____ oranges in their mouths.

    a. peeler

    b. unpeeled

Answers 1) a 2) a 3) b 4) a 5) b

23

Glossary

adjective (pp. 7, 13) – a word used to describe someone or something. Tall, green, round, happy, and cold are all adjectives.

bakery (p. 7) – a place where breads and pastries are made.

bean (p. 12) – a seed or a pod that you can eat.

chip (p. 7) – a small piece cut or broken off of something.

dough (pp. 6, 8, 9, 22) – a thick mixture of flour, water, and other ingredients used in baking.

salad (p. 15) – a mixture of raw vegetables usually served with a dressing.

verb (pp. 7, 13) – a word for an action. Be, do, think, play, and sleep are all verbs.